Traditional Farm Buildings

A catalogue written by Richard Harris to accompany
the touring exhibition *Traditional Farm Buildings*
organised by the Arts Council of Great Britain

The mediaeval tithe barn at Lenham in Kent.

Januar	*By thys fyre I warne my handys;*
Februar	*And with my spade I delfe my landys.*
Marche	*Here I sette my thynge to sprynge;*
Aprile	*And here I here the fowlis synge.*
Maij	*I am lyght as byrde in bowe;*
Junij	*And I wede my corne well I-now.*
Julij	*With my sythe my mede I mawe;*
Auguste	*And here I shere my corne full lowe.*
September	*With my flayll I erne my brede;*
October	*And here I sawe my whete so rede.*
November	*At martynesmess I kylle my swyne;*
December	*At at Cristesmasse I drynke redde wyne.*

Traditional Farm Buildings

The traditional farmstead is fixed in popular imagination as an unchanging feature of the English landscape. Few are aware that its buildings have undergone a long evolution or that they have always been subject to changes brought about by the introduction of new agricultural techniques.

To-day, when many traditional farm buildings are redundant and may soon disappear altogether, it is surprising that so few attempts at detailed study are being made. They are after all some of the finest buildings we possess and can tell us much about the culture and organisation of rural society before the onset of mechanisation.

We are particularly grateful to Richard Harris for carrying out extensive research, and for writing both the exhibition and catalogue texts. We are also grateful to Pamla Toler who took many photographs specifically for this exhibition.

Joanna Drew
Director of Exhibitions.

A limestone barn, with outshots probably intended for cattle, and a brick granary. Location unknown.

Traditional buildings of all kinds survive in large numbers in Britain, their familiar forms dominating our image of town and countryside. They are of great beauty, but they are also fascinating documents which reveal much about the development of our society. Houses, for example, express in their plan, as well as in their size, information about the culture and status of their occupants which is of value to historians. Geographers, also, find that the regional patterns formed by traditional techniques of building construction add a new dimension to the country's normal physical and political boundaries.

The buildings which served traditional farming – the much-loved old barn, the stable and cowhouse, and the humble cartshed – can make an especially valuable contribution to our knowledge. In their design they show the changing techniques and concerns of farmers, adding body and detail to agrarian history which can otherwise only be studied through written documents. In their materials and construction they have great advantages for the investigation of traditional building techniques, being relatively easily accessible and not obscured by coats of paint and plaster.

Farm buildings often present considerable problems of interpretation, however. Farming is a complex cycle and farming methods vary considerably from region to region. To some extent these variations can be predicted from knowledge of local soil and climate, and from familiarity with historical trends on a wider scale, but much nevertheless depended on the skills and interests of particular farmers and landowners. Because of this it is necessary to study whole farms whenever possible: individual buildings cannot be separated from farmsteads nor farmsteads from fields. When looking at a barn for storing corn, for instance, it is important to remember that teams of horses or oxen ploughed the land for the corn to grow and that the straw had to be made into manure by cattle in a foldyard before being returned to the land.

It is this interdependence of farming processes which gives farmsteads their fascination. All traditional farming was mixed: only the proportions vary between arable and pastoral. Each building therefore implies the existence of another which is complementary to it. If there is a barn there must be somewhere to store grain and somewhere to use the straw. If there is a cowhouse there must be a dairy, and the traditional practice of feeding the waste products of the dairy to pigs will usually point to there being a pigsty nearby. If there is a shelter shed for cattle there must be a foldyard, and the manure made there will have been distributed on arable fields. If there is a stable for working horses or oxen there must be a shelter for carts and implements.

Animals need crops for feed, and crops need animals for manure. Humans need corn for bread and beer, and animals for milk, meat and labour. The reason for mixed farming is good husbandry and the result is – or rather, was – self-sufficiency. It is the balance rather than the nature of the operation which varies over time and from place to place. The true balance, however, may be very hard to gauge from the buildings alone. In *Farmers' Glory*, A. G. Street quotes a labourer on a Wiltshire farm consisting of sheep,

arable land and a large dairy herd: *"All we do do is run about and sweat atter they blasted sheep. We be either lambing 'em, runnin' 'em, marken 'em, shearing 'em, dipping 'em, or some other foolishness. And they can have all the grub we do grow, and God knows how much it do cost the Guvnor fer cake."* In this instance the hated animals dominated the farming cycle but the buildings would have given little evidence of it.

◂ *A Norfolk barn, timber-framed, thatched and with a porch.*

The Barn

Old barns are impressive and picturesque and therefore much admired. Being of great size they were built with care and skill, a symbol of the farm's prosperity. Now they are usually empty and disused but the threshing floor and open storage bays still retain a strong atmosphere. Every surface is covered with fine yellow dust from threshing and the smell of straw seems to become part of the fabric.

The barn was the most important working building in the farmstead, taking pride of place amongst farm buildings as well as in the public imagination. Its main functions were to give safe storage to the unthreshed corn crop, to give shelter to the threshers working through the worst of winter, and to store the threshed straw before it was used as litter and fodder for the cattle. The threshing floor, on which threshers flailed the corn, always lay across the barn between doors on each side. The larger door, often with a porch, was big enough for a loaded wagon to pass through at harvest time. The threshing floor was constructed of flagstones or timber, or of beaten earth: it had to be durable to resist the annual beating of the flails. The sheaves of corn were stored in one end of the barn, the threshed straw in the other.

The oldest surviving barns are the mediaeval monastic granges, the earliest dating from the late 12th or early 13th century, but these were more like huge warehouses than working farm buildings. From the 15th and 16th centuries a certain number of barns survive from manor (demesne) farms or those of enterprising yeomen, but by far the majority of existing traditional barns date from the 17th, 18th and

Threshing with flails. The sheaves by the door await threshing. Winnowers are at work beyond the threshers.

early 19th centuries. Many of them are buildings of three bays, perhaps 40 to 50 feet in length, the central bay containing the threshing floor and the two end bays being used for storage. This type is so common that it may be considered the standard traditional English barn.

Large barns are often reputed to have been tithe barns. While there is seldom any direct evidence for such use, the payment of tithes in kind was an important element of farming and village life and undoubtedly many of the large early barns which survive were of manorial status and must have been used to house tithes and rents in kind as well as the produce of the demesne farm itself. By the late 18th century the majority of tithes were paid in cash rather than kind.

The custom of placing the threshing floor transversely across the barn was universal in Britain and had two practical advantages: it separated threshed straw from unthreshed sheaves and it allowed for winnowing in the through-draught between the doorways. Space was needed for dressing the grain as well as for threshing: the following description of the various operations refers to the early 19th century:

Threshing, the most unwholesome of rural occupations, was practically the only winter employment.

... Threshed by the flail, the grain was heaped into a head on the floor of the barn. The chaff was blown away by means of the draught of wind created by a revolving wheel, with sacks nailed to its arms, which was turned by hand. Thus winnowed, the grain was shovelled, in small quantities at a time, into a hopper, whence it ran, in a thin stream, down a screen or riddle. As the stream descended, the smaller seeds were separated and removed. The wheat was then piled at one end of the barn, and "thrown" in the air with a casting shovel to the other extremity. The heavy grain went furthest; the lighter, or "tail", dropped short. To some of the corn in both heaps the chaff still adhered. These "whiteheads" were removed by fanning in a large basket tray, pressed to the body of the fanner, who tossed the grain in the air, at the same time lowering the outer edge of the tray. By this process the whiteheads were brought to the top and extremity of the fan, whence they were swept by hand. Lastly the corn was measured, and poured into four-bushel sacks, ready for market. The operation of dressing was slow. As the sun streamed through a crack in the barn-door, it reached the notches which were cut in the wood-work to mark the passage of time and the recurrence of hours for lunch and dinner. The operation was expensive as well as slow, costing from six to seven shillings a quarter. (Lord Ernle, 'English Farming Past and Present', 1912.)

There are two intriguing points of similarity between barns and houses which suggest a tradition common to both. Mediaeval houses were entered by a through-passage between opposed doorways, and the entrance to a house is known as the 'threshold'. Whether this means that threshing was at one time carried out in the through-passage is an open question but it certainly suggests some correspondence between the entry to a house and the entry to a barn. Perhaps it is simply that entry into a transverse passage is a fundamental tradition of buildings in this country, common to houses and barns. In some areas of Europe

barns and houses also share a common tradition, but of entry in the gable end, the barns having longitudinal rather than transverse threshing floors. The other point of comparison is that when barns have small rather than wagon-sized doorways, as they do in some parts of the country, the door invariably opens inwards, as do doors in houses. In the farm in Rosedale which is illustrated in the exhibition, for instance, all the doors open outwards except the barn door.

Barns were primarily buildings for storing and processing the crop but many examples may be found of barns which also housed cattle. In Yorkshire, for instance, it is believed that the wide side-aisles of some barns were used for cattle, and similar arrangements were certainly in use in Lancashire. Some barns in Surrey and Sussex also appear to have been designed to house cattle, but in the East and South East generally aisled barns were certainly only intended to house corn. The 'bank barns' of the Lake District are arranged so that straw can be dropped from the barn above to the cattle and horses below, and applications of the same principle can be found elsewhere. The aim of minimising the labour of carrying straw from the barn to cattle will be found to underlie the arrangement of buildings in many farmsteads.

From the early 19th century threshing and winnowing were more often performed mechanically, but this did not immediately render barns redundant. Space was still needed for the storage of straw and the threshing machine was housed inside the barn. The main change in design was that some, if not all, of the

The tithe barn at Frindsbury in North Kent.

◄ *Ashstead tithe barn in Surrey, probably late 18th century.*

A 'bank-barn' in Great Langdale, Cumbria. The upper part contains a threshing barn, with a byre and stable below.

barn would be provided with an upper floor, cattle and horses being housed below. Even in the late 19th century a threshing floor was still often provided for flail threshing of small quantities.

In their construction barns follow the patterns prevailing locally and the standard achieved (in surviving examples, at least) is usually as good as that of houses. In areas of timber framing the panels of the frame were infilled, in early examples, with split oak pales woven around vertical oak staves; left undaubed these panels permitted air to ventilate the crop in store. From the 18th century mechanically sawn boards were used instead, covering the outside of the frame. Tarred or limewashed, these boarded barns are a characteristic feature of the countryside in many areas. In other areas local stone was used, with vertical slits to allow ventilation. Brick came into common use in the 18th century and the patterns of ventilation holes in the walls vary from place to place.

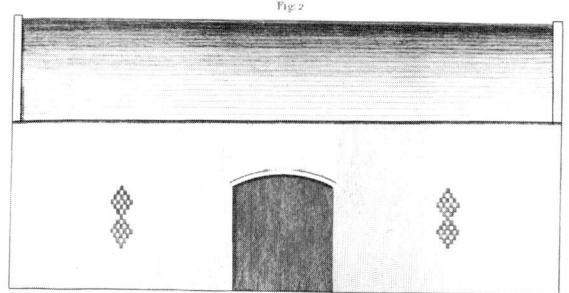

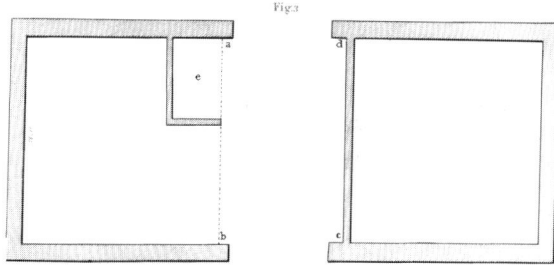

Plan and elevation of a three-bay threshing barn, from 'Communications to the Board of Agriculture', 1797. Unthreshed corn was kept in the right hand bay, with a low wall (cd) to keep it from mixing with straw being threshed. Threshed straw was kept in the left hand bay. Figure 'e' is the corn-hole, "a place for putting the thrashed corn out of the way till the whole is thrashed, or time had to clean it and put it elsewhere. This place is about 3'0 high, and covered with boards, but open on the side next the thrashing floor."

Buildings for cattle

Climate is the controlling factor in animal husbandry. While most stock could be put out to graze on pasture in the summer, overwintering in the fields was difficult in many areas both because of the weather and because of the damage done to pastureland by cattle in wet conditions. Dairy cows and working oxen were usually housed for the winter at least, tethered in stalls. Otherwise the most common arrangement was for cattle, particularly young cattle, to be kept in a foldyard. Covered yards became popular in the late 19th century, but the traditional foldyard was open to the weather, protected only by the surrounding buildings. The use of foldyards depended on a plentiful supply of straw for litter, and a reasonably dry climate.

Straw of various kinds played an important part in stock management, for fodder as well as litter. Wheat and oat straws were used for both purposes. Barley and rye straws were generally used for litter and rye straw, being hard and wiry, was better suited to yards than stalls. The straw of peas and beans, known as 'haulm', made excellent fodder. Straw used as litter was returned to the fields as manure: manure is not simply dung but a mixture of dung and straw trodden and compressed together by cattle in a well-drained yard or byre. Foldyards, in which manure was made and collected, thus had a reciprocal relationship with arable farming. The buildings associated with foldyards are open-fronted shelter sheds which cattle in the yard could enter at will. They do not have stalls or tethering rings but simply a feeding trough or rack on the back wall. The shelter shed may be freestanding or

The end gable of a cowhouse in the Home Farm at Beamish, Co. Durham.

◄ *Two long horn cows tethered in their stall at the Acton Scott Farm Museum in Shropshire.*

Foldyard and shelter sheds in the Vale of York.

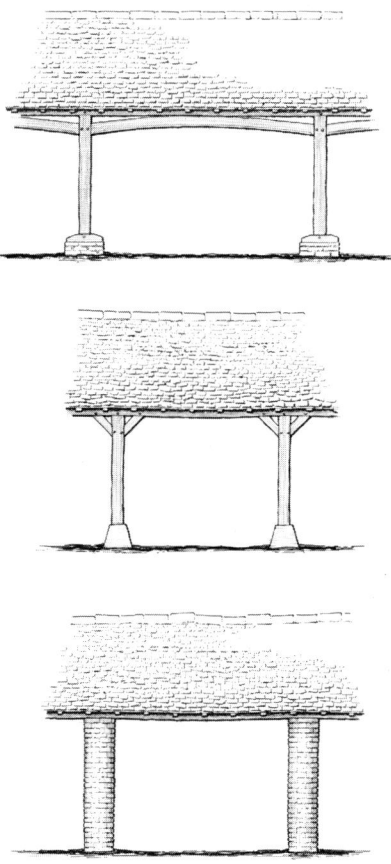

form part of a range of buildings on the side of the foldyard. A common traditional arrangement was for the shed to be a lean-to against the barn. In some areas (particularly Devon) an open-fronted hay-storage loft (the 'tallet') was provided above shelter sheds to form a building known as a 'linhay'.

Most traditional farmsteads include a cowhouse, containing stalls in which cows were tethered, fed and milked. Cowstalls usually allow for two animals between partitions, although sometimes the stalls are omitted and each beast is simply tethered to a post. At the rear of the stalls there is always a drain and a passageway for removing manure to the foldyard, and there may also be a feeding passage in front of the stalls from which the racks or troughs were filled. The arrangement of the rows of stalls varies, sometimes lying across the width of the building and sometimes along its length. If they lie across its width there may either be a single doorway for the manure passage or two, three or more doors for the manure and feeding passages.

Examples of different forms of open fronted shelter shed.

Granaries

Grain was perhaps the most precious and carefully guarded farm produce: it supported life by providing bread and ale, and it was the seed which would produce next year's harvest. Grain yields remained surprisingly small, due to the many inadequacies of traditional farming methods, until the improvements of the 18th and 19th centuries. Because of its value and comparatively small bulk, grain was traditionally kept in an upper room of the farmhouse, sometimes with external access. Most grain would be consumed on the farm or in the village, although on larger farms a proportion was left over as a cash crop.

With increased yields and the general tendency for self-sufficient farming communities to split into independent profit-making businesses, the provision of a purpose built granary became more common in the 18th century. A granary is essentially a storage box which is protected against vermin and damp by being raised off the ground. It may either be on staddle-stones (the mushroom shaped stone supports which were sometimes also used to keep cornstacks off the ground) or raised to first floor level above an open cartshed or a stable. Granaries on staddle stones are found mainly in the South and East, whereas other types were built in all parts of the country. Because of the importance of protecting the grain, granaries are usually very carefully constructed. The interior may be plastered throughout, with a floor composed also of plaster or of overlapping feather-edged boards.

Storage bins for grain inside the granary shown opposite.

◄ *A small granary on staddle stones, in Surrey.*

A 'field-house' in Yorkshire, isolated in upland meadows and pasture.

A granary built over a cartshed, late 18th century.
Reconstructed at Avoncroft Museum of Buildings, Worcestershire.

Storage of hay

While climate determined the way in which stock were kept in each district, the availability of winter feed determined how many animals could be kept over the winter. Hay was traditionally the main winter fodder and was stored either in stacks or in lofts above the animals. In the late 18th century it became common in some areas to provide covered accommodation in the form of large open-sided barns ('Dutch barns'). These vary mainly in the material used to construct the supporting columns which may be of timber ('pole barns'), stone, brick or iron. A few examples can be found of hay barns with roofs which can be lowered gradually to maintain maximum protection, an arrangement which is very common in some other areas of Europe.

Stables and cartsheds

As draught animals oxen were sometimes preferred to horses. They cost less to feed, were less liable to sickness and injury, and were steadier, although slower, at pulling the plough. Their advantages were not clear-cut, however, and discussion of the relative merits of oxen and horses for ploughing was a hardy perennial in the farming press until the mid 19th century.

Horses were expensive and stables for a team of working horses only became common on ordinary farmsteads in the 18th and 19th centuries: many still survive from that period. Horses were usually kept in single stalls. In order to allow space for grooming, horse stalls were wider than single cow stalls and the stall divisions higher and stronger. A loose-box is often found within or attached to the stable, and provision was made to hang harnesses either on a wall opposite the stalls or in a separate tack-room. Because of the value of horses, stables are often larger, cleaner and better built than cowsheds, and have a spacious loft for hay or grain. A corn-chest may be found opposite the stalls. Stables usually had windows, in many cases one on either side of the doorway: it is often said that grooms needed light for playing cards as well as for attending to the animals!

Sheds for wagons, carts and implements were the simplest buildings of the farmstead: as with stables and granaries, most examples date from the 18th and 19th centuries. They were open-fronted or open-ended and seldom fitted with doors. Often they contained an upper floor for a granary or other storage. They usually face away from the farmyard or are placed just outside the main range of buildings for ease of access.

A modern version of the traditional cartshed.

◄ *Working horses in their stable on a Humberside farm.*

Buildings of pastoral farming

Many aspects of traditional life in England fall into a pattern of two contrasting zones: the 'highland zone' to the north and west, and the 'lowland zone' to the south and east. Traditional agriculture in the highland zone was based on predominately pastoral farming and in the lowland zone on arable. The differences are due to soil, climate and topography but they are reflected in many other aspects of life, indicating a basic cultural division of the country.

House plans and traditional building construction, for instance, can be analysed in terms of these zones, and settlement patterns and farmstead groupings show a similar distinction. Arable farms need at least one important building – the barn – and village co-operation was important because of the high value of a team of oxen for ploughing. Therefore the barn tended to dominate arable farmsteads, while village communities dominated economic and social life. Basic pastoral farming, however, needs no major buildings. Cattle were housed in byres, and the barns were small, reflecting the smaller relative importance of the corn crop. Farmsteads tended to be isolated or grouped in small hamlets, with the buildings joined together in a linear arrangement (although all kinds of plan can be found). Because of the lack of straw and the high rainfall, foldyards are seldom found in upland pastoral farmsteads. Cattle were housed in winter and put to pasture in summer.

As well as these differences of grouping, some specifically 'highland' building-types can be identified. The best known of these is probably the 'longhouse', in which house and byre are built under one roof but separated by a through-passage running across the building. In some examples the passage seems to have been the entry for cattle as well as for humans, but more often it was either the feeding passage or simply a means of access from the house to the byre, the entry for cattle being a separate external door in the wall of the byre. Longhouses are found mainly along the western fringe of the highland zone, in the Lake Counties, the Welsh Marches and the South West. Some longhouses are mediaeval, but there are also many later examples.

The 'laithe-house' is a building-type which is mainly associated with upland pastoral farming in Yorkshire. The local term 'laithe' means a combined byre and barn, and a laithe-house is a dwelling house attached to a laithe. They differ from longhouses in plan because there is no through-passage and usually no inter-communication between the house and the laithe. They are later in date than longhouses, the first known examples belonging to the late 17th century. Throughout much of the highland zone it is common for houses and farm buildings to be joined together in a line, and the laithe-houses of the Yorkshire Pennines may be seen as a special instance of this more general pattern.

◂ *A Yorkshire 'field house', probably 19th century.*
The upper entrance leads to the hay-mow, the lower to the byre.

A farmstead in the North Yorkshire Moors, serving a predominately pastoral farm.

A third building type characteristic of upland pastoral farming is the 'field-house'. These are usually two-level buildings on sloping sites distant from the farmstead, in which hay from the surrounding meadows is stored above and fed to the cattle below. They are, in effect, isolated manure factories designed to minimise lifting and carrying of hay and manure in hilly country, equivalent to the 'out-barns' found in arable areas which typically consist of a threshing barn and a shelter shed enclosing a foldyard.

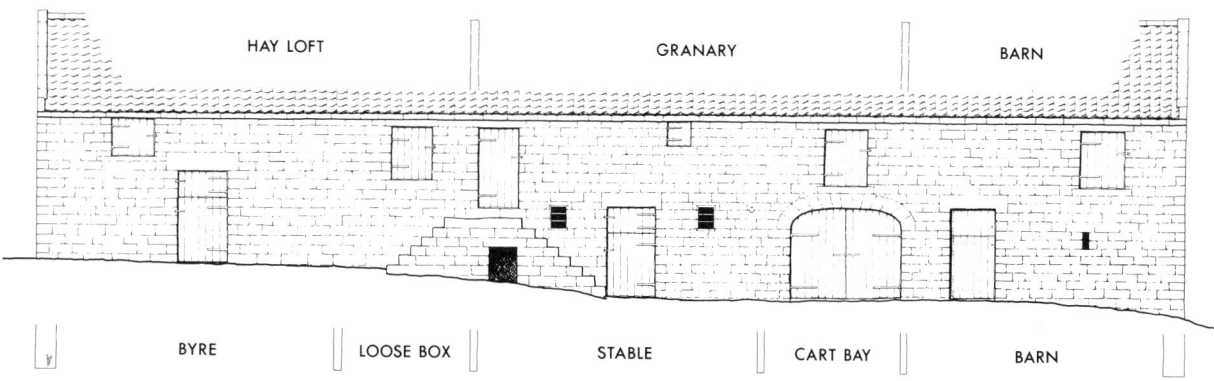

Elevation of the farmstead shown opposite.

A new road formed during enclosure of the Lincolnshire parish of Swallow in 1806

Enclosure and the Design of Improved Farmsteads

Despite the sporadic enclosure of common lands which had taken place since the Middle Ages, English farming remained in essence a co-operative pursuit until the Enclosure Movement of the late-18th century. Agriculture had traditionally been based on open fields and common rights held by the farmers of the village. The purpose of enclosure was to extinguish common rights in exchange for a fixed holding of land so that each farmer would farm only his own fields, enclosed from the common fields. The result was an improved standard of agriculture because the better farmers and landlords could now carry out experiments and improvements which would have been impossible under the open-field system. However, much suffering and waste occurred when cottagers found themselves with a tiny plot of ground, often difficult to cultivate, instead of the right to graze a sheep or cow on the commons; many, unable to scratch a living from the soil, sold their holding and became landless labourers.

Often a new farmstead would be built in the middle of a newly enclosed farm and the resulting buildings are interesting as they reflect precisely the pattern of agriculture of the time. So many farm buildings were built in this period that it is always worth searching for an enclosure award when investigating a farm. However, because of the large amount of capital involved, many 'enclosure farmsteads' were built up over a period of years, so it is not often that the Act of Enclosure will accurately date all the buildings of the new farms.

In the second half of the 18th century farming became fashionable. The involvement of gentry and nobility led to the best contemporary architects being commissioned to design splendid new farmsteads, and in the same period many pattern books were published containing designs for farmhouses and farm buildings. The schemes were sometimes lavish – 'Coke of Holkham' claimed in his will to have spent half a million pounds on new buildings – and aimed to dignify traditional building forms by the application of fashionable architectural styles.

These developments did not win the unqualified approval of contemporary writers. In his report to the Board of Agriculture, 'A General View of the Agriculture of the East Riding of Yorkshire', 1812, H. E. Strickland wrote: *But the folly even of an overbuilt farmhouse is surpassed by that of an ornamental one. What, indeed, can be so absurd and devoid of taste, as a Gothicised farm-house, or Castellated cottage? To the credit, however, of the landowners of this county, such incongruities seldom occur.* Arthur Young, also, was typically outspoken in his advice to young farmers in the '*Farmer's Calendar*', 1804: *The fashionable sheep-shearings, farming clubs, societies, &c. render another remark not absolutely unnecessary: a steady, careful old farmer may not be the worse for mixing a good deal in company of much higher rank than his own; but a young man with a small degree of animation may suffer by it. His eye and his mind become insensibly accustomed to objects and habits of living to which he was before a stranger; to steer clear of all imitation is not a very easy task, but it is an extremely necessary one: if after an excursion which has carried him into great, and what is called good company, he returns home not quite so well*

The corn barn and cartshed at Swallow Grange, Lincolnshire.

satisfied with home as he was before, he has contracted a taint that may be worse than the scab among his sheep.

The farmyard layouts of the new and improved farmsteads of this period usually followed a well-established pattern. The buildings were ranged around a courtyard, the barn forming the north side flanked by cowhouses, loose-boxes and shelter sheds opening onto the foldyard. Stables and wagon sheds generally faced away from the main yard. An alternative arrangement sometimes adopted was for the barn to form the centre, with other buildings grouped round it or attached to it.

In the mid 19th century another phase of expansion and building took place, the period of so-called 'High Farming'. The designers were now specialist engineers rather than fashionable architects and the buildings were consequently more workmanlike. Most jobs on farms were still done by hand and the principle underlying the designs is usually the avoidance of unnecessary labour in fetching and carrying fodder and litter. In this period the barn gradually ceased to be an open storage and threshing shed and became a complex combination of spaces for machines, storage and livestock.

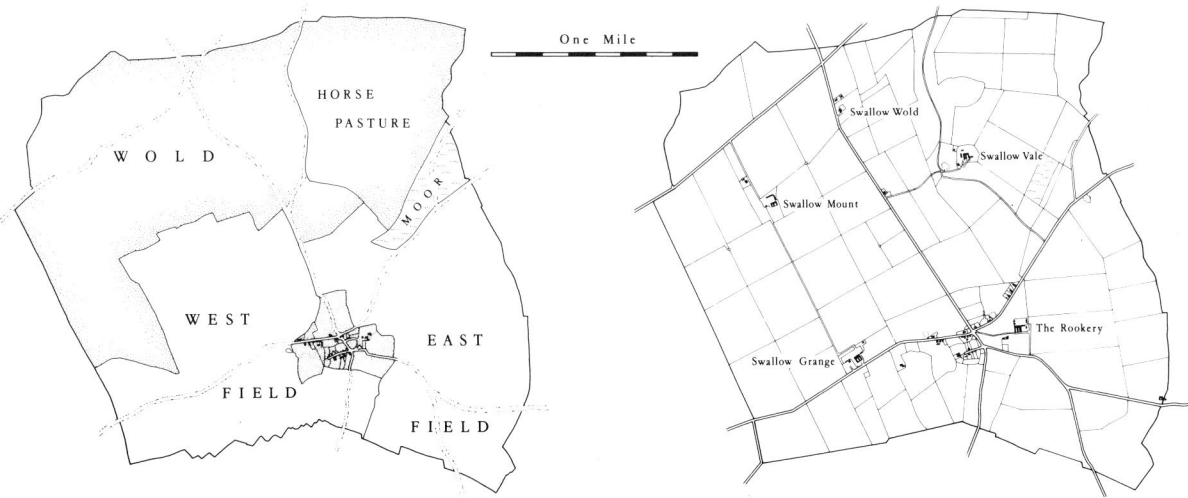

The open fields of the Lincolnshire parish of Swallow

The same parish divided into separate farmsteads following enclosure in 1806

Power and the Modern Farm

The death-knell of traditional forms of farm buildings was sounded by the introduction of new sources of power and new machines to be driven. In a sense the cart came before the horse: new machines were invented first and driven by improved applications of the age-old power source, animals.

In 1788, when Andrew Meikle patented his threshing machine, threshing was at last successfully mechanised. The immediate impact on farm buildings was the addition of horse-engine shelters to the sides of barns in which the new threshing machines were housed. Many of these circular or polygonal shelters still exist: they occur most often in counties which had a mining or industrial base, both because the necessary engineering expertise was therefore available locally and because the alternative winter employment in industry lessened resistance to mechanisation of what had been the main winter labouring job available in the countryside.

In the mid 19th century steam power became available to farmers. If the farm was large enough a stationary engine was often installed: the engine house, built against the side of the barn, is easily recognisable by its tall chimney. As well as powering the threshing machine, the engines were used for a number of processes of feed preparation: hay and straw had to be cut into chaff, turnips and potatoes sliced or pulped, oats bruised and beans ground. On smaller farms a contractor would be hired to thresh the crop, and many 19th century barns were provided with a hard-standing for the annual visit of the steam engine and threshing box.

Horse-powered threshing an engraving published in 1866.

In our century electricity and the internal combustion engine have completed the process of change. Corn is now threshed on the move at harvest time: grain is transported directly to driers and silos, and straw bales can be stored in field stacks or in Dutch barns. The threshing barn is completely redundant. Mechanisation and improved standards of hygiene have also altered the management of dairy herds and other livestock. No traditional farm building can now be used efficiently for the purpose for which it was first designed.

In the first half of this century farming suffered a long depression caused mainly by foreign competition. Money for new building was short. Old and outmoded buildings often had to be adapted to the demands of new methods, equipment and regulations, and there was much patching, repairing and improvisation. Because of this the majority of farms changed only

◄ *On this Kent farmstead grain is dried and stored in modern bins, but the old barn is still used for storing hay.*

slowly from their 19th century appearance. Since the 1950's, however, there has been a considerable amount of renewal and new forms of building have become a common sight in the countryside.

Many people regret that the traditional countryside is changing so quickly but they forget that change is nothing new. The late 18th century age of enclosure and improvement and the 19th century advent of steam power both brought fundamental changes to the appearance of farms and the way of life in the countryside. It is easily forgotten also that one thing remains constant in farming: the skill and experience needed to farm well. To a farmer a useless building has always been an obstacle to good farming and a drain on his resources. Constant renewal is therefore necessary, but it is unlikely that today's concrete and asbestos sheds will ever win our affection as traditional barns and farmsteads did.

◄ *Kentish aisled barn, still in use for storage.*

Recording Farmsteads

There are many aspects of traditional farmsteads which are not yet understood, particularly the regional variations of building types. The study of vernacular architecture in general has progressed rapidly since the 1950's, and much attention is being given to Britain's heritage of early industrial buildings, but farm buildings have fallen uncomfortably between the two disciplines. Destruction of old farm buildings is, inevitably, proceeding apace and it can be argued that we have missed by forty years the ideal opportunity for their study.

Much still remains, however: each English parish may contain anything from five to several hundred farmsteads, of which a good proportion retain some, at least, of their older building stock. In studying farms the challenge lies in the richness of the material. While it is fairly easy to identify the various types of buildings on a farmstead it is much more rewarding if the buildings can be related to the land and the methods of husbandry. It is always valuable to walk into the fields as well as round the farmyard. The lie of the land and the quality of the soil are important, of course, but the trees and hedgerows, ponds and streams, fords and gates, are all part of the history of a farm.

It is best to concentrate on a single parish or group of farms and to combine field-work with documentary research. Estate maps and surveys, tithe maps and enclosure maps, often available in the County Record Office, contain much relevant information. Fieldwork on the farmstead should include an examination of all the buildings: the small buildings near the farmhouse

are often neglected but can provide the links between the farm and the domestic economy. Pigsties, henlofts, goosepens, dovecots, oast-houses, corn-drying kilns, dairies, wash-houses and slaughter-houses all played a vital part in the farming process.

Some researchers suggest that only 'traditional' buildings should be recorded, with a terminal date at about 1880, but there are arguments against this. In disregarding modern buildings it is possible to miss valuable clues to the earlier pattern of farming, whether in half-concealed remains of older buildings or in the natural tendency for the use of particular areas of the farmstead to remain constant. Furthermore, few farms have experienced a complete break in farming technique: understanding a farm's present use can add to the validity of the interpretation of earlier buildings. Most important of all, much of the information about the use and development of a farmstead will come from the farmer himself. It is tactless for a visitor to show great interest in the ramshackle barn but to be blind to the modern buildings to which the farm owes its continued existence.

The list of books on old farm buildings is astonishingly short. '*A History of Farm Buildings in England and Wales*', by Nigel Harvey, is a useful general study, especially as it continues the story past the usual 19th century 'cut-off' for traditional buildings. '*The Development of Farm Buildings in Western Lowland Staffordshire up to 1880*', by J. E. C. Peters, is an extremely detailed and comprehensive survey which is interesting both in itself and as a basis for comparisons in other regions.

'*An Illustrated Handbook of Vernacular Architecture*', by R. W. Brunskill, illustrates traditional building construction and contains an excellent summary of the various types of farm buildings. '*Recording the Buildings of the Farmstead*' is a booklet by the same author, published by the Ancient Monuments Society, which puts forward a procedure for rapid and systematic recording.

Some unpublished theses and a small number of specialist articles could be added to this list but, bearing in mind that farm buildings make up a very substantial proportion of surviving traditional buildings in this country, it is evident that much research remains to be done. Unless circumstances change, almost all of it will be done by amateurs. National bodies such as the Royal Commission on Historic Monuments recognise this and are anxious to give all the help they can. Farm buildings have surely played too great a part in our history to be allowed to vanish without their story being told.

◄ *Outside an early-19th century farmstead in Humberside.*

Acknowledgements

The author wishes to thank the following people and institutions for their help in preparing this exhibition and booklet:

The Acton Scott Farm Museum
Roy Armstrong
C. J. Bond (Oxfordshire County Museum)
Dr. R. W. Brunskill
Hereford and Worcester County Record Office
Kent County Record Office
Leeds Archives Department
Lincolnshire County Record Office
David Michelmore
Geoff Morton
National Monuments Record
Chris Page and Catherine Wilson (Museum of Lincolnshire Life)
Stephen Price
Rex Russell
Strickland Teesdale
Dr. S. Ward (Museum of English Rural Life, Reading)

Photograph Acknowledgments

Richard Harris 15, 17, 29, 39
Museum of English Rural Life 4, 25, 35
Francis Pugh 12
Pamla Toler 6, 10, 11, 14, 16, 18, 19, 20, 22, 24, 26, 28, 30, 32, 34, 36, 38 (and end papers)
Ben Weinreb 13

The 19th century barn and cartshed at Hasholme Carr Farm, Humberside.